# Dear Triyana

## Insights and Advice to Prepare You for College

## By Treshan Nilaweera

Copyright © 2025 by Treshan Nilaweera

All rights reserved.

No portion of this book may be reproduced in any form without written permission from the publisher or author, except as permitted by U.S. copyright law.

Cover design by Paige Jalosinski

*Dear Reader,*

*This is a series of letters I wrote to help my sister prepare for her freshman year.*

*I hope they help you as well!*

# Subject: Opportunity Cost

Dear Triyana,

I received a LOT of advice before starting my freshman year of college.

The trouble was, most of the advice I received was cliché, redundant, or contradictory:

- "College is the best time of your life."
- "Take advantage of every opportunity."
- "Don't work too hard."
- "Go to your professors' office hours."
- "My professors weren't that helpful."
- "Your GPA doesn't matter after college."
- "Get a 4.0 or else you'll have trouble later."
- "Don't procrastinate."
- "Don't stress about your career. You have time."
- "Get a summer internship—it's essential."
- "Make as many friends as possible in the first week."
- "Your friends from the first week won't last."
- "Just be yourself."
- "College is where you find yourself."

It was all well-meaning. I am very lucky to have had people around me who were practically jumping at the opportunity to give me their advice.

But it was a little hard to keep *track* of it all. If two people contradicted each other, who exactly was I supposed to believe? If two people disagreed with each other, how could I know what was right?

I think I had trouble because all these cliché phrases lack **depth**. They tell you *what* to do, but don't explain *why* you should do it. All these statements are true, but they don't give you the complete picture.

Initially, I wrote this book in the same limited format.

- "This is how you can survive your first week."
- "These are the types of clubs you should join."
- "This is how to get a freshman-year internship."

I tried to tell you how to live your life. I told you how to study, how to make friends, and how to have the best college experience.

But... that format felt shallow and rigid.

Despite growing up in the same place, we are *very* different people. You are driven while I am patient. You like chocolate while I like vanilla. You like parties, loud music, and doing things for the plot; I enjoy books, ignoring my text messages, and quiet nights in.

Beyond that, you are already equipped with **a lot** of life skills you need.

You have been taking classes, making friends, and discovering yourself for practically your entire life. Sure, there are things you can improve on, but the point of going to college *is* to improve those things.

If you came in fully capable, what would be the point?

So, instead of lecturing you, I want to show you what to *expect* in your future. Instead of a book of advice, this is a book of *insight*. It's a compilation of what I noticed, what I felt, and what I experienced. The embarrassing failures, invigorating successes, and constant mind-bending bouts of confusion.

You see, I view university as a greenhouse for dreams.

It's a nutrient-rich environment teeming with connections, resources, and opportunities that can make **any** vision possible.

Want to start a business? Colleges will throw money at you through Shark Tank-like competitions. Want to explore the world? Colleges have robust study-abroad programs that'll send you to London, France, Singapore, China, or god knows where else. Want to get wasted and party for four years? Colleges have enough alcohol to drown a small country.

Anything you want to achieve, anything you want to try, anyone you want to be, is possible through your university and its resources. Modern colleges have moved past basic education. Instead, they are **launchpads**, with all the resources, connections, and time to help you build your ideal life.

Oddly, this breadth of opportunity is what I struggled with the most.

If there are so many opportunities, how do I know which one is the best one to take? When I walk through one door, how many others close? When I make a choice, how many future possibilities are lost? What if I wake up in twenty years and realize I did it all wrong? What if I wake up tomorrow and find I already missed the chance to do it right?

The cost of joining a fraternity (besides humiliation and alcohol poisoning) is not dedicating time to that club you liked. The cost of studying for your calculus midterm is missing out on that rave your friends went to. The cost of majoring in engineering is not being able to major in art, english, or business.

This only becomes more complicated as we scale the problem up. The cost of pursuing a financially lucrative consulting career might be losing out on sleep and freedom in your twenties. The cost of starting a family might be giving up dreams to travel the world. The cost of making a real impact in the world might be peace of mind and the ability to live a simpler life.

I've spent a **lot** of time thinking about this. I don't regret my freshman year at all, but I think I could have done a better job navigating college and navigating myself. The goal of this book is to equip you with the tools and knowledge needed to get a head start in navigating both.

Here is a list of the letters I wrote to you. They are limited by my own perspective, but I think you'll find them interesting:

**Preparation** - A letter covering the main preparation steps that need to be taken before your freshman year, including what to pack, finding a roommate, and registering for classes.

**People** - This letter discusses the types of people I encountered at BU. The scope of this letter extends past the student body, highlighting professors, advisors, and alumni.

**Adulting** - I found "adulting" to be both a pain and surprisingly engaging. This letter outlines my journey stumbling into adulthood: figuring out how to take care of myself, file taxes, do laundry, and all the other little challenges that come with being an adult.

**Direction** - A letter exploring the nature of goals and executing them. In this letter I list the goals I set for myself during the beginning of freshman year, discuss how I approached them, and pull insights and lessons from how things turned out.

**Community** - Finding a sense of community can be deceptively hard for college students. This letter discusses the communities I was a part of, as well as how I dealt with feelings of isolation and loneliness.

**Illusions** - This letter explores my own self-doubts. It discusses the lies I told myself and how they held me back from being happy.

**Self** - This letter tackles the common question, "Who am I?" It addresses the absurdity of the question, and how I built up and defined my sense of self over my freshman and sophomore years.

**Absurdity** - A short conclusion letter reflecting on my college experience as a whole. It offers my answer to how to deal with conflicting college advice and opportunity cost.

These letters are modular, with smaller sections listed at the top. Jump around to whatever section you find the most interesting and relevant. Good luck!

Our parents' favorite child,
Treshan

# Subject: Preparation

Dear Triyana,

I think navigating college is a lot like fighting a Hydra.

The Hydra is a monster from Greek mythology famous for having several dragon-like heads. Each time you cut off one head, two more grow in its place. Every little win is always tied to a new challenge.

Like fighting a Hydra, every success in college can often lead to new challenges.

- You passed that class? GREAT, now take a harder one that includes calculus.
- You were admitted into that club? GREAT, now here is a list of things you've got to do to stay in it.
- You got an internship? GREAT, now start applying for next year.

It's exhausting. But it's also exhilarating.

There's always something *new* around the corner—another challenge, another adventure, another chance to grow. And that's what makes college so compelling.

But admittedly… It can get really tiring.

Since fighting the Hydra is unavoidable, then let's make sure you are **prepared to win.** We can't control how the Hydra will attack, but we CAN control the armor you are wearing, the location of the battle, and the people who walk beside you.

There are several steps you can take in the summer before freshman year to set yourself up for success.

Will any of these steps solve all of your problems? No.

Can they make your life a lot more pleasant? Absolutely.

- Inventory
- Finding a Roommate
- Choosing a Dorm
- Class Registration

# **Inventory**

I like to consider myself low maintenance, so initially, I didn't think there'd be much to bring when moving into my dorm.

This perception of myself was then immediately shattered as we struggled to close the trunk of our SUV.

I mean *seriously,* where did all this stuff come from???

I think I tend to take for granted the comforts I have when living at home. Soft mattresses, easily accessible outlets, and clean shower floors don't really *exist* in college dorm rooms.

There is a standard list of items that most people bring to college. Our mom will likely remember most of them, but here is a table of the items I found to be the **most** useful.

| Item | Why I recommend it |
| --- | --- |
| Mattress Topper | Freshman dorm mattresses are basically bricks. |
| Shower Shoes | Communal showers are Petri dishes for every disease known to man. **Do not let your feet touch the floor.** |
| Toiletry Bag | I was lucky enough to get a locker, but if you are burdened with a communal bathroom, a toiletry bag is useful for bringing items in and staying organized. |
| Medicine Bag | Holds standard stuff from Band-Aids to allergy meds to cold medicine. You *will* get sick, so you might as well be prepared. |

| | |
|---|---|
| Hangers | Not a necessity, but if you wear a lot of sweatshirts, flannels, or jackets, it's nice to have them hanging versus diving into drawers. |
| Power Strip | The outlets in the room aren't always in convenient places. A power strip with a long wire makes it easy to plug in everything you need, anywhere you want. |
| Two Umbrellas | I accidentally left my umbrella at home over spring break... |
| Bed Risers | If your bed is low to the floor, then I highly recommend that you loft your bed. This gives you SO much more space. |
| IKEA Bags | These babies are your most versatile friends for carrying things. They made moving in infinitely easier, and they double as a laundry hamper. |
| Laundry Hamper | Bring a laundry hamper; it's lame to use an IKEA bag as one. |
| Fan | My dorm didn't have air conditioning. Need I say more? |
| Command Strips | An easy way to hang up items without destroying the walls and paying a fine. |
| Clothes | Bring clothes for at least a week and a half (probably more). Make sure to consider the weather conditions. Will it be cold? Hot? Wet? Dry? <br><br> Note that you can cycle clothes for the weather based on how often you are able to go home. If you know you are going |

| | |
|---|---|
| | home for winter break, you don't need to bring a heavy winter coat for fall. |
| Lysol | Wipe down your room before you start unpacking. University janitors do a great job, but do you really want to risk it knowing other college morons used the room before you? |

Beyond just practical items, I brought a lot of sentimental and personal items. Were these necessary? No. Did they make my life measurably better? Yes.

When fighting Hydras, one must *always* consider their mental health.

In general, girls' rooms tend to be more personalized than boys' rooms. But that is not a hard rule. For instance, one of my neighbors was really into anime and had his walls plastered with One Piece posters and other decorations from his favorite shows.

The brilliant thing about your dorm is you can kinda just do whatever you want with it (as long as you aren't bothering your roommate).

Here's a list of personal items I brought. This might help you start thinking about what you might want to bring:

| Item | Why I Brought It |
|---|---|
| A Whiteboard | I **love** whiteboards. They are good for studying, good for thinking, and good for explaining ideas. They are also *very* cheap compared to how useful they are. |
| Barbells | It was my intention to "get built" over my freshman year.<br><br>This did not work out. |

| High School Yearbook | My yearbook was genuinely a nice thing to have on days when I was a little bit sad or tired. The messages inside were really sweet and helped pep me up when my confidence was down. |
|---|---|
| Monitor & HDMI Cable | I like working with two screens, so I set up a monitor I could plug my laptop into. Very helpful when taking notes on a reading or video. |
| Books | I wanted to get back into reading over the course of freshman year, so I brought a large stack of books to keep me occupied. I am happy to say the stack got smaller as the year went on. |
| Travel Mug | I'm a big tea drinker, so having a mug with a lid that I could take on the go was useful for keeping myself satisfied. |
| Plush Japanese Cat | A friend of mine gave a plush cat to each person in our friend group as a keepsake for college. She swore she'd hurt anyone who lost it.<br><br>Needless to say, I still have the cat. |

# Finding a Roommate

Roommates are like family; you can't really hide from them.

Since they live in the same little box as you, your actions will almost *always* affect them, and vice versa. You will experience them at their best, and they will experience you at your worst.

I feel that having a good roommate is *more* important than having a good dorm. A bad dorm can be tolerated: if it's dirty, you can clean it; if the temperature is wonky, you can get blankets or fans; if it's far from campus, you can wake up earlier and listen to music on the walk. There are very clear actions you can take to accommodate your circumstances.

But arranging your life around another *person* is a lot harder. Different sleep schedules, opinions of cleanliness, and comfort with "visitors" can all be causes for conflict. If your roommate dumps all of their dirty laundry on the floor, *you* will be living in that laundry. If you drop food all over the tables, *they* will be living in that muck.

I would like to note here that a good roommate doesn't need to be your friend. In fact, being a friend doesn't necessarily mean someone is a good roommate. Just because you can laugh with someone doesn't mean you'll like the time they go to bed. Just because you can confide in someone doesn't mean you'll be able to tolerate the fact that they loudly chew.

A good roommate is someone who is empathetic. Who minds their own space, communicates well, and sets and understands boundaries.

Before locking in my freshman year roommate, I made sure to confirm a few basic living things (general time to go to bed, stance on overnight guests, etc.) to make sure that there were no obvious pitfalls between us.

That all being said, having someone who is a good roommate AND a good friend is an amazing experience.

I have been *so lucky* that both my freshman and sophomore roommates became my very close friends. They both have brilliant, engaging personalities, a fascinating wealth of life experience, and match my sense of humor. Living with them has changed the course of my life in so many ways, and it's hard to imagine my college experience without them.

The actual process of finding a roommate is admittedly strange—kind of like dating. "Will you be my roommate?" is a bafflingly vulnerable question to ask someone you met three days ago over the internet.

What most of my friends ended up doing was going on Instagram and cold messaging students in their year. For each grade level, most schools have these "newly admitted" pages on Instagram, where incoming students post a little bio about themselves in hopes of finding friends or a roommate.

I got very lucky: the very first person I talked to ended up being my roommate. It was easy to connect because we both had experience with writing and publishing, which gave us common ground to build on.

We had a month or so of talking before making a phone call to finalize the roommate selection. We couldn't meet up because he was from California (which is a bit far from Jersey), but it was nice to have been able to have a real conversation with him before we committed to living together.

If this weird dating-like roommate selection process isn't working for you, then don't worry about it. Random roommate selection is always an option and can lead to great outcomes. My friend who went to McGill got a random roommate who ended up being one of her best friends.

In the event you find yourself with a bad roommate, there are avenues available to you. Good, honest communication usually smooths over minor issues, and RAs are a decent resource to help moderate roommate conflicts.

In the worst case, you can transfer rooms or swap roommates. One of my friends transferred right at the beginning of her second semester, so it is possible to escape a bad situation during the school year. It's just an annoying and tedious process to move.

Additionally, a lot of people switch roommates from their freshman to sophomore years. My old roommate ended up going off campus, so I roomed with my friend from Greece for my sophomore year. So at the very, very worst, you only need to survive a single year with a bad roommate.

A quick thing to note is that room selection for the next year rolls up surprisingly quickly. At BU, it's in March, but if you plan to go off campus, you might need to start as early as November or December. Apartment hunting is a complex process in itself and should be approached earlier rather than later.

When managing a set of ever-growing challenges, a good roommate can be a great resource for support, or at the very least not make things worse. If you have the time, try to play the roommate finding game. Reach out, engage with people, and try to find someone you click with. Just remember, it's not the end of the world if you don't magically find a new best friend to live with.

# Choosing a Dorm

To stick with this extended Hydra metaphor, your dorm is basically your campsite. It's where you go to recharge, nurse your wounds, and rest for the next round. It also has the potential to introduce new, incredibly infuriating challenges if you choose badly.

As such, it's worth doing some research and fully understanding your options.

There were five main things I took into account when picking my freshman dorm:

- Quality
- Location
- Bathrooms
- Height
- Culture

**Quality:** At BU there are three main dorms for freshmen: the Good Dorm, the Quiet Dorm, and the Bad Dorm. These aren't the *only* buildings freshmen can find themselves in, but more often than not, a BU freshman will live in **one** of these three.

I ended up living in the Bad Dorm.

I think we are spoiled at BU because, at least in my opinion, all our dorms are good. Even our worst dorms have big closets, desks, lights, fans, heating, and windows. The upperclassmen dorms have more space and kitchens, but the freshman dorms are all relatively similar to each other.

Despite this, there is still a hierarchy among the freshman dorms. Whenever I tell someone I live in the Bad Dorm, their expression is always a mix of grief, pity, and superiority.

Which I think is completely unwarranted because the Bad Dorm **is not that bad**.

I don't know what you were *expecting* for your freshman dorm, but I was expecting a room that made solitary confinement cells feel *spacious*. I was expecting dark corridors, flickering lights, and to be breathing enough asbestos to get lung cancer.

Instead, my dorm building had a baffling amount of space; most rooms came with a fan, the closets were huge, there was a water dispenser on every floor, staff cleaned the bathrooms every morning, and the all-you-can-eat dining hall was **inside** the building.

Yes, the other dorms had all of these things, but not in a way that was significantly better. Just because your beds are lofted (which I'm pretty sure is because you have *less* space) doesn't mean that your little shit-box room is better than my little shit-box room.

In my experience, talk about "dorm quality" is often very skewed.

People compare dorms relative to each other, so your college's stereotypical "bad dorm" may actually still be pretty good when looked at objectively. I think the key here is to have reasonable expectations. You definitely shouldn't tolerate things like mold, bugs, or exposed wires. But if your dorm is safe, warm, and cozy, then I think it's doing its job.

**Location:** Location matters. The difference between a fifteen-minute walk and a five-minute walk may seem small, but when it's below freezing or raining or scorching, you WILL feel the difference.

My dorm was near the center of campus. I liked this placement because it was easy to get everywhere. I could roll out of bed for classes in the morning, reach all the dining halls in just a few blocks, and there were at least five coffee shops in an eight-minute radius. Living near my classes also meant that it was easy for me to chill in my room whenever I had a break between classes.

Now my dorm wasn't close to *everything*. The frats, the gym, and the shopping districts were all about a fifteen-minute walk away. But, in terms of accessing BU day-to-day, being in the center of campus made commuting easy.

A bad location at a city school like BU isn't a big problem because we have a relatively small campus. But with big state schools like Rutgers or University of Michigan, distances can mean a lot more. I have a friend at the University of Michigan who was dormed a half-hour drive away from her central campus. She needed to take a thirty-minute bus ride to get to her classes, and she said the distance hampered her ability to feel a part of and connected to her university.

**Bathroom Style:** There are two main bathroom styles in dorms: communal and suite-style.

Regardless of where you live, you will likely have to share a bathroom with other people. Communal bathrooms are shared by everyone on a floor, while suite-style bathrooms sit between two rooms and are shared among a small group of students (usually four).

Communal bathrooms have the potential to be very dirty because you are sharing them with forty or so other college-aged morons. Vomit, urine, and other bodily substances (ahem) are **very** possible biohazards in communal bathrooms.

I was lucky that both my bathrooms were relatively clean. The worst mess I've seen is a couple of wet paper towels and occasionally vomit outside the door. What's nice about communal bathrooms is that the janitors (bless their souls) clean them on a regular basis. This means that with a little time, any mess magically disappears.

Suite-style bathrooms, on the other hand, are less likely to be badly polluted because there are fewer people using them. However, there is no janitor to clean up the messes you make, so **you** are responsible for maintaining your own bathroom. This means scrubbing the bathtub, replacing toilet paper, unclogging the toilet, and everything else that comes with making a bathroom usable.

**Height:** I like waking up to natural light, and I like looking out the window a lot. Higher floors are obviously better for these two things.

The only downside with living on a high floor is the elevator wait time. My dorm specifically almost always has at least one elevator broken. This causes long elevator wait times and even longer lines. Often, I'd just opt for the stairs instead of waiting in that line.

This was a big issue during my freshman year when I had to walk up twelve flights of stairs to get to my room. While my calves may have never looked better, this was not a fun daily experience.

**Culture:** Dorms are often stereotyped with cultures. The Good Dorm is considered more social because the athletes (i.e. extroverts) live there, and it is closer to the frats. The Bad Dorm is considered to have a more "academic" and club-focused culture since it's at the center of everything.

But that does not mean that people from the Bad Dorm don't go to parties—there is a mass exodus every Friday night—and that does not mean people in the Good Dorm aren't driven, studious people.

Culture is good to *consider* because you spend a lot of time around your floormates. Being in alignment with your dorm's culture makes it easier to make friends, meet new people, and generally make your life more enjoyable.

At the same time, it's not the end-all, be-all. Colleges are so big that you can find *someone* you'll click with practically anywhere.

# **Class Registration**

It was a little jarring to go from high school, where 90% of my classes were mapped out for me, to college where choosing classes becomes a gladiator-style free-for-all.

For every major, there is a list of classes you need to take, but it is up to **you** to schedule them properly.

- **It's on you** to hit all of your general education requirements.
- **It's on you** to ensure that you have the right prerequisites for the course you are interested in.
- **It's on you** to ensure you have space for that economics minor you wanted.

There are academic advisors who can help you, but they are catering to hundreds of students and can easily make mistakes despite their best intentions.

Most schools have pages on their website that tell you the exact requirements you need. For example, I googled "Questrom School of Business BSBA" and got a list of classes I needed to take.

For your first semester, you'll also likely get an email from the academic advisor's office, which will have extra information. You are practically guaranteed to get the freshman year classes you need because they are usually big lecture-hall style courses, and no one else is really taking them.

My freshman year's class lineup consisted of basic classes and general education classes.

Basic classes, despite being introductions, are also often weed-out courses. Paradoxically, these classes can feel harder than higher-level courses because they are *actively* challenging your dedication to your major. They often have more busywork and are more time-consuming, even if the content isn't that hard.

General education classes have different names at different schools. Basically, these are classes outside of your major that your college wants you to take to make you a more well-rounded person. At BU, they are called "Hub" courses, but your school will have its own specific name. Because of the Hub program, I've taken music, history, and philosophy classes, despite primarily being a business major.

**The Registration Process**

One thing to note about registration is that you may not get your ideal schedule. You are racing a few thousand other students, equipped with nothing more than a registration date, time slot, and a dream. Be prepared to deal with suboptimal circumstances.

At my school, registration is staggered by seniority—seniors register first, followed by juniors, sophomores, and finally freshmen. This means that many classes are filled up by the time freshmen get the opportunity to even register.

Again, this probably won't be an issue for introductory-level courses; however it will affect the electives you are able to take. For my freshman registration, I had a list of six elective classes that I was interested in, and I didn't get any of them.

Your registration portal might allow you to prepare multiple potential schedules. For example, BU always allows you to create A, B, C, D, etc., plans in the event you don't get plan A.

I recommend spending some time on the portal **before** your registration time slot. This allows you to plan your schedule at a relaxed pace instead of frantically picking classes during registration.

When choosing the sections for my classes, I prioritized two main factors: **timing** and **professor quality**.

**Timing:** I preferred classes that started and ended as early as possible. I'm fine waking up early, and I love having the whole afternoon and evening to myself. I knew that if I had late-morning or afternoon classes, I'd sleep in and burn most of my day.

I also tried to avoid classes with long time blocks, instead opting for classes that met more frequently but in smaller chunks. I spread my classes over the entire week so I only had to do a little each day, but not everyone is like that.

One of my friends managed to get all his classes on Tuesday and Thursday. This meant his Tuesdays and Thursdays were *incredibly* long, but he had Mondays, Wednesdays, and Fridays nearly completely off.

**Professors:** Not all professors are created equal. Tools like *RateMyProfessors.com* are popular for comparing and contrasting them. These reviews give insights into a professor's teaching style, strengths, and quirks.

Personally, I ended up prioritizing my time slot over the quality of my professor. This sometimes left me with professors who weren't ideal and meant I had to learn more on my own. This is a trade-off you'll have to weigh for yourself—what's more important to you: an ideal schedule, or the best professor?

Finally, before spring semester registration in freshman year, I highly recommend sitting down with your academic advisor to map out a four-year plan. A four-year plan is just an outline of all the classes you need to take. It helps you make sure that you've accounted for all of the required courses you need to graduate.

This is by no means a final schedule. You can change it whenever you want. But having this plan greatly simplifies your class registration process in every semester after your first one. Plus, when I sat down with my advisor, I found out I could graduate in three years instead of four due to my AP credits, which is saving me a LOT of money.

-----------

Take your time with the tasks above, because the choices you make will affect you for the entire year. Doing things early, even just a little early, will make your life so much easier in the future.

When the Hydra's heads are bearing down on you and you have three upcoming finals, two projects, and four club events to go to, you'll be grateful that you already sorted your class registration months before you needed to think about it.

It can be frustrating to do work in the summer, especially during your senior year when you are practically checked out. But getting ahead of things will make a major difference in your stress levels during the year.

Love,
Treshan

# Subject: People

Dear Triyana,

It's very easy to feel *small* in comparison to my school. For one, the place is **big**. Even a smaller city campus like mine has *hundreds* of buildings scattered around everywhere. This isn't high school anymore where everyone can more or less exist in the same space; colleges sprawl across miles of land.

Beyond that, it's easy to feel small when compared to the *legacy* of the school. The history of the institution. The mystery and grandeur of the knowledge locked inside. The connotations and values that are all tied to the name.

But in reality, the school isn't that impressive at all without its students. The buildings are empty shells, the knowledge is just scribbled lines, and the name is but empty sounds. All these things are given meaning, given life, because of the people inside the school.

My college is a beautifully cosmopolitan place, with all sorts of colors, nationalities, opinions, strengths, weaknesses, personalities. Boston University's legacy is a patched-together mismatched quiltwork of personalities woven together into a single identity.

I didn't realize how much diversity in the community would *matter* to me until I got here. Everyone is just so absolutely unique and interesting. From the professors to the students to the advisors to the staff. Everyone has something interesting to say, or something interesting they do, or something interesting they want to do.

There is a peculiar feeling of *movement* I get when I go back to my campus, especially at the beginning of the year. There is so much excitement and energy; it's as if the place is buzzing and alive, which I suppose in a way it is.

As cliché as it sounds, the school is really just its people. People who decorate the buildings with expressions of themselves. People who advance knowledge inside its walls. People who justify the value of the name.

There are four major categories of people I have interacted with at my school. Each one of these groups has more color, depth, and personality than I could ever hope to capture on paper. I am simply trying to give a little insight into each of these groups based on my experience.

- Professors
- Alumni
- Advisors
- Students

# Professors

I didn't really think about professors when I was applying for colleges. I just assumed that at a certain point, all professors would be pretty good.

Looking back, this was a little naive.

Professors don't have too much control over the **content** you learn as a freshman. Introductory curricula are pretty limited, and there are only *so many* basic economics, business, or biology concepts. The laws of physics don't change between schools. Gravity works just as well at Harvard as it does at Bergen Community College.

What they do have control over is how that information is **filtered** and **presented**. No class can cover *everything* equally, so what a professor chooses to emphasize—or ignore—can make or break your understanding.

My two favorite professors so far have been my Management Organizations (MO) professor and my Accounting professor.

My MO professor was animated and friendly. On the first day of class, she ran the only icebreaker activity that I have ever seen actually work. Usually I find icebreakers tedious and ineffective, but somehow through clever rules and sheer force of personality, she had the entire class talking and engaged. In just a few minutes she established a strong class culture that persisted for the entire semester.

On the other hand, I didn't actually *like* my accounting professor at first. He was an older guy who was so soft-spoken that he had to use a microphone. Plus he had an odd teaching style built largely around cold-calling, which meant I was always on edge in his class.

However, over the course of the year, he managed to do something I thought impossible: he made me genuinely appreciate accounting. He prioritized student *understanding* instead of memorization, and he led me to appreciate the brilliance of the *system* of accounting and how it stores information.

On the other hand, I have had a few… less-than-ideal professors. More often than not, I find the issue isn't that the professor doesn't know their subject, but rather they have trouble conveying that understanding to their audience.

My statistics professor was brilliant; you could see that the concepts were simple to him and that he genuinely loved the subject. The trouble was his presentation of the material. He explained technical details and formulas, but often skipped over the general concepts.

I've taken a statistics class before and also know a little Python, so I was in a better position than many of my classmates. Still, at the midpoint of the semester I found myself genuinely lost.

If the quality of your professor is really important to you, the website Rate My Professors (*ratemyprofessors.com*) is a really helpful tool for picking professors.

Beyond the classroom, I often go to my professors for career and life advice. In a way they are like living libraries. All of my professors had industry experience and incredibly colorful and interesting lives. In office hours, they were able to use their great stores of knowledge and experience to help me solve my specific problems, whether it's a class concept, internship search, or research opportunities.

***This*** is the reason to go to office hours. Not because you want to "butter up" your professor for a better grade or because you are looking for a good recommendation letter. Sure, those are potential byproducts, but I believe that the true value of office hours is in your professors' insight versus other more material benefits.

I visited my Business Ethics professor very early in freshman year to ask questions about his career. Our conversation moved to networking, and right on the spot he helped me build a LinkedIn profile and connect to our alumni portal. Those two tools have become *VERY* useful to my life since then and were pivotal to getting a freshman year summer internship.

I visited my Management Organizations professor because I was spiraling about my career. I didn't know where to start, I didn't know what I wanted to do, and my self-doubt got so bad that I couldn't understand why anyone would want to hire someone like me in the first place. Over a few weeks she helped me through an exercise called *Reflected Best Self,* which helped me identify personal strengths and start identifying potential career paths. The exercise calmed me down and boosted my confidence.

I visited my Writing Seminar professor recently to learn more about the book publishing world. I love creative writing and it would be a dream come true to get my book traditionally published. I just didn't know where to start. Even though I had been out of his class for two semesters and wasn't even an English major, he was more than willing to sit down and help me get my head on straight.

For anything you are doing—case competitions, projects, clubs, internships—professors are a fantastic source of information and can help you along in big ways.

## **Alumni**

Intellectually, I knew that the alumni of the school are a great resource for my career. I mean, it's not what you know, but who you know, right? Everyone always talks about alumni opening doors at big companies or connecting students to great opportunities.

But at the same time, I didn't register how *powerful* alumni networks actually were until I started reaching out to them.

Universities are decades, if not centuries, old institutions. Every year, the university churns out thousands of graduates, who then spread out around the globe working everywhere, from nonprofits to startups to Fortune 500 companies.

The brilliant thing is, because you are from the same school, you can cold-email *any* of these individuals and have a MUCH better chance that they'll respond. I've had the privilege of talking to Deloitte Innovation Consultants, a JPMorgan Vice President for nonprofit banking, Head of Business Development for a stone quarry, and more just because I reached out and asked for 30 minutes of their time.

It's not guaranteed that an alumnus will answer your message, but your chances of success are much higher than with a normal cold email.

Despite their abundance and the value they bring, alumni networks are an extremely underutilized resource. The first alumnus I talked to said I was the fifth person to reach out in **fifteen years**.

The main two ways I connected with alumni were over LinkedIn and BU Connects (my school's internal alumni portal). Both these tools have a bunch of settings and search features that can help you find alumni in the companies or industries you want to learn more about.

The main thing to remember is **don't be shy**. At first I felt a little weird reaching out to these random working adults. But I have largely found alumni extremely accommodating and generous with their time. Just make sure to be polite, cordial, and timely. They are more than willing to help you learn and grow.

Leveraging my school's alumni portal allowed me to create an internship opportunity for myself during the summer after my freshman year. Applying for internships during my freshman year was frustrating because most internships look for juniors and I didn't have all that much on my resume at that point.

After several rejection letters, I decided not to waste my time sending futile applications and take a more creative approach. I built some skills in AI prompt engineering, created a pitch deck, and sent some cold messages to alumni. Through this I created my very own paid internship. I'll detail more about this in my **Direction** letter.

If there is something you are trying to achieve, a certain career you want—a project you are working on, a certain gap in your knowledge you want filled—I highly recommend seeing if there is an alumnus somewhere that might be able to help you. There is no guarantee that they'll answer or solve all your problems, but it genuinely can't hurt to try.

# The Advisors

I struggle with asking for help. I would rather power through an issue and figure it out myself than ever ask for advice. This is categorically dumb, as usually a fifteen-minute conversation with someone more knowledgeable than me makes the problems so much easier to deal with.

An adjustment I made during freshman year was reaching out to resources and mentors when I didn't know how to approach a problem. One of the most easily accessible resources was advisors.

Advisors, similar to professors, are living libraries. They just focus on topics related to life rather than academics. There are several types:

**Academic Advisors**: These advisors help you navigate the academic resources within the school.

Their services are surprisingly necessary. Universities have become so big and provide so many opportunities that I found it difficult to sort through everything my major offered.

Near the end of my freshman year, I sat down with my academic advisor and planned out a schedule for my next few years. In this meeting, I found that I had enough AP credits to graduate in three years instead of four, and we developed a plan to help me reach that goal. Having a plan and general idea of which classes I need to take each semester has made my class registration process so much simpler and more straightforward.

**Career Advisors**: These advisors help you navigate through the internship and job market, and I recently met a really good one. His name is Scott, and he is AMAZING. I get unnecessarily anxious about my future and tend to freeze up when dealing with anything related to my career. Scott helps prevent this by giving me direct, actionable steps. After every meeting he sends an email tackling what we have discussed, providing internship opportunities, potential alumni connections, and career events.

Beyond that, it is extremely reassuring to have someone validate **my** visions for a potential future. He isn't trying to guide me towards a specific career path or impose his ideas on me. Instead, he tries to help me figure out what I want out of a job and develop a path that is both authentic and financially stable.

**Initiative Mentors**: "School Initiatives" is a pretty broad category. In this case I'm referring to advisors you get access to through a particular program or project that you are associated with.

During my freshman year I joined an entrepreneurship fellowship where I was connected with a BU alumna who does product management at Warner Brothers. She was so absolutely cool and she is one of the people who inspired me to become a student entrepreneur.

My college has a First Year Success Program designed to help facilitate the transition into freshman year. I became friends with my business school's First Year advisor and she helped me navigate the school as a freshman. Beyond that she is also a big reason why this book exists.

Early in this book's conception, I approached her with this idea. She helped validate and mold the idea, even going so far as to pitch it to her superiors to try to get it funded through BU. While that plan didn't work out, she still went above and beyond in helping me, and this idea wouldn't have grown to what it is without her.

**Older Students**: I was accepted to both Boston University and Northeastern. When I was deciding between these schools, I reached out to high school alumni at each school to learn more about the student experience.

The BU student I reached out to adored the school. She is genuinely a big reason why I ended up picking BU over anything else.

Since that conversation we have met up once or twice every semester or break to catch up. She is in the same major as I am, so she gives me tips on classes, professors, and her own challenges. Beyond that, our conversations always devolve into bigger-ticket topics like what we want the future to be, relationships, and personal goals.

Overall, my BU experience is measurably better because of her advice and company, and this is equally true for all other older students I have become friends with.

One thing to note is that I have had great experiences with my advisors; *however,* that is not true for everyone. Some of my friends were screwed over by their academic advisors and needed to take summer classes. Others have had career counselors who simply didn't care enough to be involved. A few experienced dramatic falling-outs with students they once saw as mentors — even as older siblings.

Advisors are great resources, but at the end of the day you will have to live with the results of your decisions and actions. Go to them for perspective and assistance; don't expect an advisor to solve all your problems for you.

# Peers

I constantly find myself in **awe** of the other students at my school. Everyone is just so... interesting? fascinating? amazing? I don't think there is a word for what I'm trying to say here.

Now, it's not that everyone is perfect. College students are still human and are subject to the same pettiness, problems, and nuances of every other human. It's not like I vibe with everyone at my school, and there are definitely people I don't really care to be friends with.

But at the same time, there is just a *depth* to college students. Even if I don't click with someone, there is still something interesting and respectable about them. Some hobby, or passion, or dream, or achievement that adds color and dimension. We can have completely different priorities, life experiences, and personalities, but I somehow can still find a reason to be in awe of them.

My roommate from last year has traveled the world, started several successful businesses, and has a work ethic that could put machines to shame. My current roommate is a national Greek windsurfing champion with the mind of an Athenian and the athleticism of a Spartan. My Russian friend in computer engineering used to manage a sizable YouTube channel, directs short films with BU organizations, and builds rockets in her spare time.

I know an Alaskan aspiring personal finance guru who has backpacked across South America and is one of the most genuine and sociable people I have ever met. I get coffee with a philosophy and neuroscience student from Hong Kong who manages to reconcile faith, science, and philosophy into amazing, nuanced insights. I get lunch with a computer engineering New Yorker who manages the scariest-looking calendar I've ever seen while still finding time to be more reflective and emotionally aware than I ever could hope to be.

Biomedical engineering students who raise money for water systems in Kenya, yet somehow still have a more vibrant social life than me. Computer Science Boy Scouts who have camped atop mountains and seem to know something about everything. Fine Arts students who take pictures at concert venues and organize sustainable art supplies recycling and donation programs. Accounting students who captain esports teams and fix cars in their free time. International Business students who have literally traveled and lived everywhere from Brazil to Ukraine to Dubai.

Everyone. Is. Just. So. Cool.

Meeting all these cool people inspired me to expand myself and **be more.** It inspired me to be more ambitious, smarter, kinder, and to enrich myself with experiences, goals, and hobbies.

This perspective, this growing understanding of what life could be, has equally been one of the most valuable and detrimental lessons I have learned in college.

What's fascinating is that, despite all these differences, we can all relate and connect on the fact that we are students. Everyone has to wake up for classes. Everyone is struggling to build their future. Everyone is figuring themselves out and trying to grow.

Despite being so absolutely different, we are all also absurdly the same, and that allows us to laugh, talk, and learn together.

-----------

Love,
Treshan

# Subject: Adulting

Dear Triyana,

Adults have a frustrating habit of welcoming me to the "real world" whenever I have to do anything "adulting" related. Commuting for work, filing taxes, making tough decisions, etc. It's as if pointing out my struggle like a bleak Captain Obvious makes theirs just a *little* bit lighter.

I find this **VERY** annoying, but unfortunately I do see where they are coming from.

There is an oddly perverse pleasure in watching someone stumble at a challenge you've mastered. It makes me feel smart, and proud, and just inflates my ego overall. So tragically, I can see myself doing this to the next generation when I'm older, even if I find it incredibly frustrating now.

It's also... scarily *easy* to forget how it feels to be young.

I'm only twenty, but I can't really remember how I viewed the world in middle school. Sure, I can tell you that I vaguely remember being tired, excited, lonely, etc. But I can't *explain* those feelings to you. I can't explain what it **felt** like to be in middle school.

Was it crushing? Like the sky pressing down on my shoulders? Or was it energizing? Like a sharp bit of cold wind that wakes me up? What did it feel like to be excited at that age? What did it feel like to be sad?

What's even more interesting is that my current perspective recolors my prior experiences.

When I think about middle school now, I remember it being safe, carefree, and easy. But... I don't think my eleven-year-old self found it all that simple. My new perspective and state of life are actively rewriting my previous ones.

This is all to say that it's very easy for someone older than you to forget how it feels to be in your shoes. It's easy to remember the strategies, the events, the outcomes, but it's a lot harder to remember the feelings.

So, this letter is dedicated to silly, stupid, and obvious challenges that are easy to overlook in hindsight. Challenges that you will definitely face, definitely struggle with, and definitely grow to master.

# **Adulting**

There are all these little "adulting" tasks—these coming-of-age moments that can be really, *really* annoying.

The trouble with living alone is that there is no one else to handle vacuuming, managing trash, and buying toiletries. There is no one to remind you to register for your classes or to remind you to swap your laundry from the washer to the dryer. It's all on **you**.

Now, none of these "adulting" tasks are particularly hard. You'll get the hang of them pretty fast. It's just good to be aware since they have an annoying habit of appearing out of nowhere.

- Doing laundry correctly
- Ironing clothes
- Deep cleaning (vacuuming, dusting, carpet cleaning, etc.)
- Filing taxes
- Evading taxes (kidding)
- Answering summons to jury duty
- Registering for the draft
- Memorizing your Social Security number
- Booking travel (buses, trains, planes)
- Packing properly for buses, trains, planes
- Finding a barber
- Washing dishes
- Removing old food from the fridge
- Cooking
- Job applications
- Job interviews
- Professional emailing
- Budgeting
- Registering for credit cards
- Paying off credit cards
- Etc.

I've compiled a table with tips on a few of the "bigger-ticket" tasks I encountered while learning to "adult." Unfortunately, at the end of the day, it's on **you** to learn and manage these things for yourself.

At some point you'll be an adult, so you might as well start learning now.

| | Tips and Tricks |
|---|---|
| Laundry | I always set a timer so I don't forget to move or pick up my laundry when a cycle ends.<br><br>Forgetting laundry is not only discourteous (remember, you are sharing the machines with *everyone* else in your dorm building), but also imprudent.<br><br>Students *can*, and *will*, dump your clean clothes on the floor in order to put theirs in, so make sure to be on time. |
| Filing taxes | The IRS has a set of tools called "Free File" that assist you with your taxes completely for free. I've found that they make the process so much simpler and straightforward.<br><br>You can find these tools at https://www.irs.gov/filing/irs-free-file-do-your-taxes-for-free |
| Jury Duty | If you are a US citizen and live in Massachusetts for over fifty percent of the year, you are eligible to be called for jury duty.<br><br>Massachusetts is notorious for roping students in jury duty, but the rules vary state by state, so make sure you are aware of your state's policies.<br><br>You can postpone and change the date so it best fits into your schedule. I've also heard of people getting fully out of it, but I haven't figured out how to do that yet. |
| Job Applications | The best thing I can recommend you do about job applications is look into the process early. Recruiting |

|  | cycles are getting earlier and earlier, with some finance internships being locked in over a year in advance. You don't *need* a freshman-year internship, but doing a few applications will help you learn the process, and be more confident in the future where internships become more critical. Also go to your college's career center; they can be incredibly helpful. |
| --- | --- |
| Booking Travel | I use an aggregating site called Wanderu when I'm booking travel to and from Boston. This helps me compare all possible buses and trains in a single app instead of searching every provider separately. Similarly, you can use sites like Expedia for aggregating flights. In my experience, sites like Wanderu have slightly more inflated prices than the providers themselves. As such, I tend to use Wanderu to compare options, and then I go directly to the transport company to actually buy the ticket. |

# **Physical Health**

When I was in middle school, there was a running joke that I was a robot.

This was because I was decently clever, highly "logical," and *always* seemed to be doing something productive. I remember there was a lot of debate about whether I was powered by batteries or solar panels or nuclear fission.

Unfortunately, I have recently discovered that I am very much NOT a robot.

Instead of electricity, I'm *actually* powered by food, sleep, and the occasional shot of caffeine. I get sick. I get tired. I get sore.

Despite my grandest delusions, I am still human.

At first, it was very easy to ignore my physical health during college.

I'm young, so a few lost hours of sleep or a skipped meal didn't affect me too much. At the time, there were just *so many* things happening that were worth disregarding my physical health for. (Late-night conversations, parties, cramming for tests, etc.)

But at some point, I started to feel negative effects. Sleeping inconsistently meant I woke up feeling miserable, and struggled to fall asleep. Eating the *same* chicken sandwich every day made me sick of the dining halls and eating in general. Skipping fencing or the gym to doomscroll on social media made me feel lethargic and exhausted.

The real killer was when I got sick.

Not only did being sick hurt my physical health, it also hurt my mental health. While I was sick, I didn't want to see anyone, get up from my bed, or do any of the work I had to do.

Maintaining good physical health (outside of illnesses) is so easy it's almost boring. It requires consistency and prioritization. Sleep at the same times, eat at the same times, exercise at the same times.

Because maintaining health is boring, it's easy to overlook. It's boring in the way brushing your teeth is boring. It's boring in the way dusting a shelf is boring. It's boring in the way doing laundry is boring. But it's important if you want to feel energized and happy.

Also drink water. No, Starbucks does **not** count as proper hydration.

# Mental Health

I found it really easy to feel *bad* about being sad in college.

Here I was, funded by my parents' hard work, in a privileged environment of learning that many would kill for, surrounded by opportunities to do anything I ever wanted. What right did I have to ever be sad? Or tired? Or stressed?

The trouble is, when I started thinking like that, my mental health only got **worse**. Instead of talking to someone, I would berate myself as weak. When I was tired I would push myself until I got sick or crashed. When I was stressed I repressed my feelings until they built up and paralyzed my actions.

There is definitely merit in the stiff-upper-lip philosophy. In taking accountability for your actions. In focusing on being grateful for all the good things in your life, instead of harping on the bad.

But that is **not** the same thing as denying your emotions altogether.

My philosophy is that nearly all emotions are valid, but how we act on them is not. The caliber of a person is determined by how they act *through* negative emotions.

When you are angry, do you lash out at those around you or do you go for a cooling walk?

When you are sad, do you wallow in your own self-pity or do you ask a friend for tea and company?

When you are stressed, do you let your panic rule you or do you take a break to calm down?

I find managing my mental health is about mastering *measured* reactions. It is equally bad to completely deny your feelings as it is to wallow in self-pity. There is **always** a choice in the middle that is the healthier option to take. Be sad, but get your work done. Be sad, but talk about it with a friend. Be sad, but try your best to enjoy a quiet day by yourself.

If you broke your knee, I wouldn't ignore it and tell you to walk it off. Equally, I wouldn't panic and give you heart surgery.

Why should broken emotions be any different?

Like physical health, the actions that maintain mental health are kinda boring, and honestly feel a little silly.

Affirmations sound stupid until you realize you *are* feeling more confident. Meditation is a waste of time until you realize you *are* feeling calmer. Gratitude journaling feels basic until you realize you *are* feeling more positive and happy.

Personally, I like going on long walks and sitting on a park bench (yes, I know I act like an eighty-year-old man, I have heard it a million times).

Every Friday, I would go on a walk, get a hot chocolate, and watch the sunset, and every Friday I would go back to my dorm feeling just a little happier and calmer.

I'm not saying you have to act like your grandfather but I ***highly*** recommend finding something that rejuvenates you. This can be literally anything from knitting to listening to music to a weekly activity with your friends. Ritualize it, and give yourself something to look forward to every single week.

Also, you'll most likely need multiple rituals that make you feel better. Going on a walk helped when I was stressed or confused, but didn't really help when I was feeling lonely.

I can't say what you should do to make yourself feel better; that's unique to each person. But I would counsel **against** treating social media as something that rejuvenates. Social media is entertaining, and it can be great to physically rest as I rot in bed. But more often than not, I exit doomscrolling sessions feeling more mentally exhausted than going in.

Of course, if it works for you, then scroll away. But I recommend being intentional and figuring out what **actually** rests you versus what just fills your head with cheap dopamine.

## **Spiritual Health**

I don't mean spiritual in the sense of religion. I also don't mean spiritual in the sense of vibes, gemstones, or any other New Age magics.

I mean spiritual in the sense of "having to do with one's spirit." With having to do with one's morale, sense of self, or sense of purpose.

There have been times in my life where I've felt physically great (consistent sleep, food, and exercise) and mentally great (lots of time spent with friends, hobbies, and myself), but I would still feel *weird*.

I felt like I wasn't moving anywhere. Like my life didn't have purpose and that I was stagnating.

On the flip side, there have been times when I have been incredibly tired and incredibly stressed, but I was **so happy** because I was pursuing a goal that excited me. I was growing and learning, and that challenge made me feel alive.

I'm… still trying to understand this component of my health. I'm not even sure "spiritual" is the right word to describe this feeling.

But I do feel like this is a real thing, and it's worth thinking about for yourself. It's somehow related to that satisfied feeling you get when you finish a hard workout. Or the relief you feel after getting past a particularly difficult finals season. Or the excitement you feel when there is sudden, surging movement in your life.

The key to **my** spiritual health lies in creation—writings, curricula, videos, etc. Projects I can pour myself into and fully immerse myself in the creative process. Subjects that make me excited to learn and where I find myself consuming more and more information. Priorities that make hours fade away, render sleep no longer necessary, and turn doubt into an afterthought.

I don't know how to enter this "flow state." I don't know how to balance spiritual health with the rest of my life. But I think it's worth exploring and understanding.

One thing to note is that I **don't** believe maintaining spiritual health requires you to be obsessive.

Some people are able to pursue their missions with insane determination and focus, but I don't think that lifestyle is for me.

I can still feel challenged and inspired **while also** maintaining my mental and physical health. I just have to make sure I have a strong enough sense of purpose to be proud, without sacrificing the rest of my life.

-----------

What's nice about adulting is that it genuinely feels *easy* once you've done it for a little while.

A credit card is only a confusing concept if you've never had one. Using an iron is only frustrating when you've never picked one up. Prioritizing sleep only feels stupid because you've never felt the need to before.

The best thing you can do (and something that took me embarrassingly long to learn) is approach this part of your life with humility.

You are going to be the stupidest one in the room for a while, and that's **beyond okay.** Because I can guarantee you everyone in that room has been equally stupid at some point in their lives.

Eventually we'll be the wise old adults who get to laugh at how foolish these youngins are, and personally I'm very excited for when we have that opportunity for ourselves.

Love,
Treshan

# Subject: Direction

Dear Triyana,

In a way, college feels like standing at infinite crossroads. There were so *many* potential ways my life could have gone. Infinite variations of my story that *could* have happened, had I just made a few different choices.

I struggle with this sense of vastness when planning for the future, and I often need something to **anchor** myself to. I need a sense of *direction* so it feels like I'm moving towards *something* instead of stumbling around an endless sea of possibilities.

For most of my life, it felt like this sense of direction had been established for me by others.

I loved my high school extracurriculars, but I did them because they were expected of me. I love my friends, but often my friendships were established by extroverts "adopting" me into their lives. I'm so absolutely happy about the fact I went to college, but I never even considered the possibility of not enrolling in higher education.

But when I got to BU, I faced the beautiful perplexity of having no expectations at all.

Aside from keeping up my grades, I could do **whatever I wanted**. I could pick up random sports. I could learn a new language. I could travel and explore. I could play video games all day and no one could stop me.

I was granted near-full agency to explore life how **I** wanted to.

As I mentioned in other letters, I have made some amazing and terribly impressive friends at BU. I wanted to be as cool and interesting as they were, so I spent my freshman year focusing on self-improvement.

I wanted to be healthier, be better-read, work on cool projects, etc.

So, after a bit of brainstorming for a few days, I set the following goals for my freshman year:

- Do well academically (No average under B)
- Create a Design-A-Thon project worthy of winning
- Physical improvement (Description Pending)
- Read 8 books
- Build connections and communities
- 5 creative projects
- Set up a summer job or internship for 2024
- Develop a full-fledged business plan for FYIF Venture
- Have fun and enjoy freshman year

I recommend setting some sort of goals for yourself. They don't need to be specific or even particularly productive, but just having *something* to aim for helps make your life feel more intentional and directed.

I think there are three major steps when pursuing goals: Setting the goals, executing on them, and reviewing the results.

Put more plainly:

- Why set goals?
- How do we follow through?
- What actually happened?

# Why set goals?

My reason for setting goals has always been pretty simple: I am unhappy about something.

I set the goal of physical improvement because I was unhappy about being a skinny twig. I set the goal of building connections and communities because I felt lonely and isolated. I set the goal of reading eight books because I felt wholly inadequate compared to my much more well-read friends.

Being unhappy, however, isn't enough to accomplish your goals. It's perfectly possible to be very unhappy and do absolutely nothing about it. Being unhappy is the pushing action that encourages you to do something, but it's powerless without a sense of **aspiration**.

In order to set a goal, there has to be something I aspire to achieve. Something I want, something I'm inspired by.

I set the goal to create five creative projects because I wanted to be the type of person with cool creative skills. I set the goal for the biomedical engineering design competition (Design-A-Thon) because I wanted to try to invent an impactful device and win the competition. I set the goal to develop a business plan for my entrepreneurship program (FYIF) because I was enamored with the idea of being an entrepreneur.

Alone, aspiration is lofty and fleeting. I need the conviction provided by being unhappy to step out of my comfort zone and pursue my dreams.

Alone, unhappiness is frustrating and debilitating. I need the optimism and inspiration from aspiration to encourage me to take a step outside of my comfort zone and pursue my dreams.

These two ideas work together, almost like electricity or a bolt of lightning. Being in a negative or positive state isn't enough to create a flow of energy; I need two "charges" working together to inspire action.

I think the first important step is figuring out and knowing what you **genuinely want**. It's easy to have a billion things you want to do and a billion things you are unhappy about. The important question is, out of both of those lists, what matters most **to you**?

After you figure out what you want, you have to figure out the structure and wording of the goal. As cliché as it is, the framework of SMART goals (Specific, Measurable, Achievable, Relevant, Timely) is *really* helpful.

- Your goals should be decently well-defined
- You should have a way to check if you succeeded
- Your goals should be humanly possible
- Your goals should be relevant to what you want
- Your goals should have a time frame (for me it was the end of freshman year)

Don't fret too much about getting the "wording" of your goals perfect; they will evolve and change over time. Just make sure you are factoring the above considerations when planning so that the goals you set are actually achievable.

## **How do we follow through?**

Often, I will find myself chasing my goals when I feel inspired.

Do you ever have those fantastic rushes of energy and motivation that usually hit you right as you are going to bed? A surge of excitement that has your mind racing a million steps ahead, building a clear and achievable picture of what you want out of the future?

Then, of course, you wake up the next morning—that surge of energy gone and the goal seeming a lot sillier at 8am than it did at 12am.

A trap I used to fall into a lot is letting my emotions dictate whether I work towards a goal or not. I would only go to the gym if I felt like I had energy. I would only do that job application if I found the willpower to do it. I would only write that chapter if I felt inspired to do so.

What's worse is that I would **wait** until I felt right. I would wait to have the energy; I would wait to find the willpower; I would wait till the inspiration struck me.

This led to weeks or months passing with absolutely no progress. This lack of progress would make me feel worse, reinforcing my poor self-image. This poor self-image would suck my energy, erode my willpower, and stifle my inspiration, thereby creating a negative feedback loop that would lead me nowhere at all.

It took me embarrassingly long to learn that executing your goals properly has almost nothing to do with feelings, and has everything to do with habits.

It was very easy to grasp that feelings inspire actions. I'm mad, so I throw my controller across the room. I'm sad, so I sit down and cry. I'm happy, so I smile.

What I didn't grasp at first, is that **actions** also inspire **feelings**. Taking deep breaths makes me less mad. Going for a walk makes me less stressed. Genuinely smiling even when I'm sad makes me happier.

I shouldn't wait for energy to exercise, because exercising fills me with energy. I shouldn't wait for willpower to submit a job application, because submitting an application reinforces my willpower. I shouldn't wait for inspiration to write, because writing even just a little bit will inspire me to do more.

The hard part is starting. Not just the first time, but starting **every single time**. Mustering the willpower to go to the gym didn't magically become easier because I went once. In fact, after three weeks or so, it felt harder. But every day I made the decision to go, I would feel a little better about myself and a little more energized because **I was trying.**

For me, there is always this "activation barrier" whenever I start a new task. To deal with that, I rely a lot on habits and systems.

I find it's easier to make progress when I focus on the *action* instead of outcomes. A lumberjack who loves the sound of a tree falling will lose interest after a few swings. A lumberjack who loves to swing his axe can cut down an entire forest.

As of this writing, I have drafted two other books in my life. One was 144,000 words written over the course of four years. The second was 80,000 words written in just five months.

The difference? For the 144,000-word book I wrote when I felt like it. I intermittently started and stopped the project based on vibes at the moment. Instead of focusing on the page I was drafting at the moment, I would hyperfixate on the fact that I had hundreds of pages still left to write.

But for the 80,000-word book, I wrote consistently. Over the course of five months, I would sit down at the same spot at the same time and just write. Regardless of how I was feeling, or how tired I was, that writing schedule *could not change*.

By systematizing my process, I was able to make progress so much faster. Beyond that, I also just felt better about myself. I was proving to myself that I could be disciplined. I was proving to myself that I was in control of my whims.

I don't think I've ever felt more like an author than when I built writing into my schedule in such a fixed way. I don't think I've ever been more satisfied with my process than since I wrote that book.

I am far from perfect in building systems and cultivating habits. I mess up, indulge in cheat days, and stumble more than I'd care to admit. But turning my goals into processes has enabled me to make more progress, more consistently, than I ever could have dreamed of.

## **What actually happened?**

Goals help orient me. They point me in a certain direction so that when I take action, it moves me towards the things I want. The goal itself isn't the point—more so the *spirit* of the goal.

I didn't complete all my freshman year goals. I abysmally failed one, and for at least three others, I "cheated" the original definition. But in each of those goals, I made progress in the direction I wanted to.

I would like to highlight the *very different* outcomes of four of my goals:

- Physical Improvement (Description Pending)
- Create a Design-A-Thon project worthy of winning
- Read 8 books
- Set up a summer job or internship for 2024

**Physical Improvement:** I abysmally failed physical improvement. This should have been obvious by the (Description Pending) note I left for myself. I had no definition for what physical improvement meant to me; I wasn't sure how to design a system to achieve it, and it was easily the lowest priority on my list.

I maybe went to the gym to lift weights once in my entire freshman year—and even then, I only stayed thirty minutes because I was embarrassed that I didn't know how to use the machines.

I flipped the script in sophomore year. I made a covenant with a close friend of mine that we both had to go to the gym four times a week or there would be dire consequences. My Greek roommate helped build me a routine, showed me the ropes, and went with me for a week to help me set my rhythm.

I'm still a skinny twig, but I don't think I've been healthier or more energized in my life.

**Create a Design-A-Thon project worthy of winning:** This goal was for a year-long biomedical engineering competition I joined with a few friends at the beginning of the year.

The wording of this goal is very intentional. Winning a competition is often something *out* of my control. I can do a bunch of great work and create something amazing, but someone else could genuinely have something better or the judges could simply not like my project for some arbitrary reason.

So instead of focusing on winning, I wanted to focus on creating something that I felt was worthy of winning. That way I wouldn't be too disappointed if we lost the competition, but I still would strive to make something great.

My team met once a week practically every week for the entire year (systematizing our process) and we ended up building a Braille keyboard attachment for smartphones. It allows visually impaired people to type on their phone by using physical buttons in a Braille arrangement. We did this because the visual-impairment features on smartphones (while well-meaning) are GENUINELY a pain to use (something we discovered through interviews and by attending a blind technology expo).

Despite being a team of freshmen with limited engineering experience, we won second place.

**Read 8 Books:** I love reading, especially fantasy and science fiction. However, when I entered college, I somehow convinced myself fiction was childish, and that the only type of productive reading was *nonfiction*. I set this goal because I wanted to try to emulate my much more well-read and cultured friends, and be a more knowledgeable person in general.

The books I read weren't *bad*, in fact they were very insightful. But reading them was a slog. By the time I ended freshman year, I had barely read five. I am also not sure how much of the information I will actually retain in the long term.

During the summer, I picked up fiction again on a whim. I ended up reading four books within the span of a single month. I found these books to be more insightful and significant than the nonfiction I had read that same year. While the stories were *fake*, the arguments they made and ideas they portrayed were **real**. Today I read a lot more, even if it is "just" fiction.

This is one of the goals I "cheated" on. Sure, I read eight books, but the books I read were **not** in the original spirit of the goal.

However, I don't see this as a *bad thing*. Sometimes the priorities a past version of me set don't actually line up with what current me wants or what's **actually best** for me. As we grow and change, we should be allowed to evolve our understanding of what we truly are trying to achieve.

**Set up a summer job or internship for 2024**: This was the only goal on my list that wasn't established by me, but rather by my parents. Initially, I resented it for that reason.

It did not help at that time that I *hated* the job-hunting process. I hated writing the resumes; I hated writing the cover letters; I didn't even have anywhere I wanted to work, so why was I even doing this? Why was I doing all this work for something I genuinely had no interest in?

But... I also understood *why* my parents were pushing for this. I was graduating in three years, so I needed to be on a more accelerated path than the average freshman. What *felt* like a freshman-year internship was in truth, my sophomore year internship.

Even still, the standard application process felt and was genuinely futile. So I had to get a little clever.

Over winter break, I took a class on Prompt Engineering through Coursera. This was back when Generative AI was still pretty new. I learned a great deal and got a fancy "Prompt Engineering Specialization" certificate that I could put on my LinkedIn profile. Using these credentials, I cold-emailed twenty or so alumni and offered to help them leverage AI in their companies. Of the twenty, five got back to me, and I ended up meeting virtually with one of them.

After a few pitches to a few important people, I walked into the summer having created my own *paid* internship. The experience was really cool and I learned a *lot* about market research, business functions, and operations work in general. I am still a little baffled that this half-baked plan worked out, but I'm happy I put myself out there and tried something unconventional.

-----------

Love,
Treshan

# Subject: Community

Dear Triyana,

There is this weird phenomenon I noticed among all my friends during our freshman year. Everyone seems to have experienced a period of isolation and loneliness during that first year.

This seems to happen regardless of whether they have a lot of friends, a significant other, or a strong meaningful support system.

I was no exception to this trend.

Initially, I was so confused when I felt lonely because I had no logical reason for feeling it.

I had a solid network of new friends and an excellent roommate. I actively stayed in touch with old friends and only lived a few hours away from home. My classmates smiled and said hi when we passed each other in the hallways, and I was a fairly active member of my clubs.

I was not alone by any conventional meaning of the word.

So why did I *feel* so alone?

Admittedly, I don't know if I can fully explain that *feeling*, even to this day. It felt like everyone had found their place *except* me. That I was somehow doing something wrong.

I think it was a combination of the transition to college, growing up, meeting new people, FOMO, and a bunch of other little smaller issues bundled into one.

But out of all the many causes for this feeling, I think the most powerful cause was feeling like I lacked **community**.

Sure, I had a bunch of friends, but they were all individual connections. Sure, I had a strong friend group, but we were small. Sure, I was a student at BU, but I barely felt connected to the larger institution beyond my classes.

Feeling connected to a community is a different type of connection than one would have with a friend.

There is a quiet sense of *belonging* when I feel a part of a community, a sense that I deserve to be somewhere and that I'm wanted.

Back at home, I was part of several communities, though I don't think I properly saw their value at the time. Regardless of whether I was happy or sad, there was always a sense of being at home.

But when I went to college, I was suddenly estranged from the only communities I ever knew. **That affected me.**

I also had absolutely no idea how to deal with or even begin to identify this problem. I've felt lonely before, but never so inexplicably lonely that it made me confused. I genuinely couldn't tell what I was missing, and I felt so absolutely stupid for not understanding properly.

In my opinion, it takes two things to feel a part of a community:
1. Identifying with a community.
2. Actively engaging in said community.

This is perhaps common sense, but it took me *forever* to figure out.

In freshman year, I was in a state of transition. While I didn't change instantly or dramatically, I had the *option* to change. I was a blank slate, fully able to play whatever role I wanted to try. As such, I didn't identify with any particular group because I didn't identify with much of anything.

At the same time, I hadn't been at BU for all that long. I've grown up in the same neighborhood for most of my life, so I never realized how long it would take to truly feel a part of a new community.

It takes me about four to eight months to truly feel a part of something; it may be different for you. Some of my friends seem like they can connect to a group instantly or within a few weeks; others will take over a year.

Eventually, these feelings of isolation passed. I found a few groups I identified with and spent enough time with them to feel like I belonged.

It's fascinating how **many** overlapping communities you can be a part of. It's also fascinating how many communities you can *not* feel a part of despite being there all the time.

There are five communities I'm now a part of that I'd like to highlight for you.

- Class of 2027
- Questrom School of Business
- Fencing
- Hometown
- Entrepreneurship

**Class of 2027:** The first week of my freshman year was one of the most vulnerable times in my life. Not because I was brittle or fragile, but because everyone, including myself, was so absolutely open and *forward* about everything.

On the first night, my roommate and I info-dumped our personalities to each other. We talked about everything from hobbies to relationships to politics to fears.

At that point, I was a **very** closed-off person. My friends and family often spend ages trying to pry information from me, yet here I was with practically a complete stranger just chatting away.

This trend would continue with most people I met. I found myself telling and saying things that no one had a right to know given how recently we met. I found myself feeling like I had known some of these people for months, even when it had only been a few days.

There was this infectious magical buzz of excited nervous energy all around campus. **Everyone** was worried about making friends, so we were all uncharacteristically social. In a way, it felt like we were back in kindergarten—just walking up to random kids on the playground and somehow forming a friendship.

I found myself a part of a 20-plus-person friend group, and for a minute, despite the size, I felt like I belonged somewhere.

Then, of course, things started to calm down. Groups started to split, classes picked up, and everyone started to figure out their initial starting places. The sense of community that had suddenly spiked almost immediately started to fade, leaving me with an odd sense of withdrawal.

Still, even after that, it's easy to feel a sense of camaraderie with my graduating class. There is a special little resonance I feel whenever I find out someone is Class of 2027 just like me. Even with students outside of my school. A weird little sense of understanding passes between us—rooted in the fact that, despite differences in school, age, or circumstance, we share a common identity.

**Questrom School of Business**: Oddly, I didn't feel very connected to the business school despite being a business major. This is probably because I never joined any Questrom clubs or professional fraternities. Not participating in these orgs insulated me from the underlying social currents within the school.

It's baffling to me how many people from my classes know—or at least know of—each other. Fraternity dynamics, relationship drama, and interactions between organizations were all happening around me, yet I had absolutely no idea where or when any of it was taking place. I have friends in my major, but I definitely didn't feel immersed in whatever social spiderweb seemed to be unfolding around me.

Business students have a reputation for being backhanded and hyper-competitive. Questrom students are nicknamed "Questrom snakes" by the other majors and communities at BU.

But, weirdly, I haven't seen that. Sure, there is drama, messiness, and problems, but not in any way that is *particularly* unusual. Everyone I've met seems to be genuinely helpful, interesting, and nice enough. I'm not friends with all of them, but I don't feel like anyone is actively hostile. I went in expecting a viper's nest and ended up finding just... *people*.

Despite not being present in this community, the fact that I am a Questrom student is strongly tied to my personal identity.

Whenever I meet someone new, I will nearly always announce the fact that I'm a business major within the first few minutes. Whenever someone meets me, all the preconceived notions (positive and negative) of being a Questrom student are unavoidably attached to me. It's an identity that'll follow me for the rest of my college life and perhaps even beyond that.

For a little bit, I felt a sense of FOMO due to how I interacted with the Questrom community. I wondered if I should have joined a professional fraternity, or thrown myself at one of the more competitive business clubs.

But I think I'm happy with how I navigated this community so far. I have had the opportunity to work with some amazingly cool people, make some solid friendships, and learn a whole lot. At the same time, I've been able to stay out of the messiness and social games that some of my friends deal with. I think I'm okay just being on the sidelines of this community, at least for now.

**Fencing:** I highly recommend picking up a sport during your freshman year. When life gets hectic, it is *scarily* easy to vegetate inside your room.

You don't even need to be particularly *good* at the sport you choose. Just playing *any* sport can help keep you active, happier, and healthier.

Sports programs are also a fantastic source of community.

I decided to pick up fencing in my freshman year largely because I'm a geek for swords. Longswords, katanas, scimitars, zweihänder, khopeshes, rapiers, etc. If it is sharp, metal, and could be reasonably wielded by Aragorn son of Arathorn—I. Am. Interested.

I came for the swords, but ended up staying for the fantastic people. The fencing community at BU is relatively small and also *very* welcoming. We don't have a varsity team, so skill levels range from newbies who come into the club not knowing anything (like me) to veterans who have fenced for 10+ years and trained under Olympic athletes.

Everyone is friendly and helpful, so new fencers find themselves drowning in a tide of tips, advice, and strategies. However, there are also competitions and rankings, so veterans who take their sport seriously can fence against the professional teams from Brown, MIT, Northeastern, and more.

I, unfortunately, don't attend practice enough to really get good. I'm fast and occasionally pull off a cool trick, but going once a week isn't really enough to stay competitive. Due to this, I didn't feel a part of this community for a long time because I felt like I didn't have the *right* to define myself as a fencer. I thought I was too new, too bad, and too uncommitted to claim that "title" for myself.

However, just by sheer force of time, my perception of myself started to change. I'm still not the best, but that doesn't really matter as much anymore. I still enjoy everyone's company, I love the game, and in a surprising way I do feel like I belong there. I'm now very happy to say I'm a VERY amateur fencer, but a fencer nonetheless.

**Entrepreneurship:** Even before arriving on campus, I knew I wanted to get involved in the entrepreneurship community at BU. I submitted my application to a Freshman Innovation Fellowship program three months before the deadline—probably the first time I've ever submitted something early. At the time, the *idea* of being an entrepreneur excited me more than any other career path.

So I attended the Innovation Department's events; I went to community mixers; I founded a startup; I talked to countless creative, driven, and passionate people with crazy dreams; I made a bunch of very cool friends, and was a regular face at our building.

Yet despite all this, I didn't really feel *a part* of this community until early sophomore year. It took time for me to see myself as a student entrepreneur rather than just someone curious about entrepreneurship, and even longer to feel like more than just a visitor.

The defining moment was returning from freshman-year summer. I lost touch with a lot of my friends from the Entrepreneurship community over the summer months, and I wasn't entirely sure those friendships would continue into my next year.

However, coming back to the community was genuinely a wonderful experience. Everyone greeted me warmly, and it was fantastic to fully realize that these people were *happy* to see me and actually liked me being there.

Recently, I stepped away from my startup, which challenged how I defined myself as an entrepreneur. Despite that, I still feel like I am a part of and connected to this amazing community. I still love talking about audacious ideas, I still love working on creative projects, and I still love being a part of everything to do with innovation at BU.

-----------

When I was younger, I used to fear change, especially social change.

I'm an introvert and often am a little awkward when making friends. Most of my close friendships came from being connected through mutual friends, rather than me actively seeking out and connecting with new people.

But to find community, I needed to take more *agency* in my social life.

I had to go to unfamiliar places, meet new people, and try new things. I needed to accept that I wouldn't feel perfectly comfortable immediately, and that it would take time and effort to feel a part of something.

If you find your communities right away, that's fantastic—but don't be surprised if it takes more time than you expected. Be patient with yourself and with your school. You'll find your place eventually.

Love,
Treshan

# Subject: Illusions

Dear Triyana,

I often compare myself to others.

Specifically, I put my friends and peers on pedestals and use their achievements and amazingness to berate myself. I wonder if I'm spending my time properly. I constantly doubt my ability to achieve my goals.

In college, I found myself presented with a cohort of amazingly talented and fascinating people. This is, of course, an *amazing* privilege. Many of these peers are good friends, and I am very happy I met them.

The trouble with being surrounded by so many amazing people is that there are a lot of people to compare myself to.

Oddly, I didn't struggle with everyone being smarter than me from an academic standpoint. I'm decently clever but I knew some of my classmates were valedictorians, some salutatorians, and some achieved perfect scores on their SATs, and I wasn't deluded enough to believe I'd be "top of the class" compared to those guys.

Instead, I struggled with how interesting everyone's personalities and life experiences **outside** of school were. I marveled at the accolades they won, the businesses they started, the hobbies they excelled at, and the places they had lived.

Everyone was so *fascinatingly* cool that I found myself feeling very *limited* in comparison.

Initially, I was inspired. I wanted to be like these cool people. I *needed* to be like these cool people. I spent much of my freshman year trying to be **better** in every possible way. But when I failed to grow as fast as I wanted to, I started to tell myself a series of insidious lies.

I told myself I wasn't good enough. I told myself I wasn't smart enough. I told myself I lacked discipline, creativity, and plain old basic social skills. I told myself that I was doing college "incorrectly," and that there was something *wrong* with me.

Instead of being *inspired* by everyone around me, I felt terrible about myself. This bad self-esteem only made it harder for me to grow, creating a very annoying negative feedback loop.

These lies grew into grand "illusions" of sorts that warped my perception of myself for an embarrassingly long time. In this letter, I want to discuss the main two that trapped me, and how I eventually broke out of them.

The illusions are:

1. Everyone is better than me.
2. Everyone has more friends than me.

# Everyone is better than me

People are amazing—or at least I think so. Everyone always has some sort of hobby, interest, or life experience that makes them light up and fun to talk to.

At BU, there are a LOT of people who have interesting life experiences. I've met students who have backpacked across continents, started successful businesses, self-published books, dominated various sports on an international level, spoken multiple languages, and worked for big-name companies.

I labeled these students as "game-breaking" because they broke my previous conceptions of what was *possible*.

Through them, I realized there was so much **more** to do than just joining clubs or getting a degree. I realized that it's possible for people my age to be genuinely extraordinary and have a real impact on the real world.

I *really* wanted to be game-breaking. I wanted to be the person who could make friends with anyone and everyone. I wanted to be the person who traveled the world and had exotic stories to tell. I wanted to be the person who started successful businesses in college. I wanted to be the person who dominated my sport and any game I played.

But to be game-breaking requires more than just *daydreaming*. It requires the ambition to step out of your comfort zone, then the courage to follow through.

The entrepreneurs only built businesses after years of effort and experimentation. The world travelers only had cool stories because they risked uncomfortable and potentially dangerous traveling conditions. The socialites only were good at lighting up a room because they have been doing it for *so long*. Being game-breaking takes **time**.

But I didn't understand this at first.

I saw all my friends doing amazing things *so easily,* and I wondered why I wasn't good enough to be like them. I had this unreasonable expectation that I had to make something of myself in just a single semester when most of my friends started their journeys a long time ago.

What made this *worse* was that I would take someone's best trait or skill and compare that to my completely novice or average ability.

When I thought about my skill as a writer, I would take the most eloquent writer I know and compare myself to him. When I thought about my skill in public speaking, I would take the most extroverted and confident speaker I know and compare myself to her. When I thought about my ability to fence, I would take the most athletic and skillful fencer I know and compare myself to him.

It didn't matter that I could fence better than the writer, or that I could write better than the speaker, or that I could speak better than the fencer. I put myself down regardless.

I applied this thought process to every part of my life, and (surprise, surprise) I began wondering why **everyone** was better than me in "**every way**".

My biggest mistake was that I tried to be everything and everyone at the *same moment.* Instead of being patient with myself, and celebrating the progress I did make, I attacked myself for every little "failure" my mind conjured up.

It was **good** for me to aspire to be like my friends. It was **good** for me to try to improve myself. It was **good** for me to progress and grow.

It was **not good** for me to tear my self-esteem apart in the pursuit of growth and progress.

## **Everyone has more friends than me**

Every college student struggles with their social life at some point.

Either they feel like they don't have enough friends, or that the connections they've made weren't strong enough, or that they're not with the right people.

College students struggling socially is such a cliché that it's almost boring, and yet it is still worth discussing.

My biggest struggle was that **everyone** seemed to have more friends than me. They all seemed to know each other and seemed to be going out and having fun without me. Everyone seemed to have this social stuff figured out, which made me feel terrible as I was the only one left struggling and scratching my head.

This notion is, of course, silly.

There was a one-hundred-percent chance that there was at least one other person who didn't have everything figured out. It was impossible for everyone to know *everyone*, so I was just experiencing confirmation bias. Plus I had talked about this issue with enough friends from high school to know they were struggling too.

But when I watched people go out on Friday night while I stayed in… logic felt irrelevant.

I genuinely felt like there was something *wrong* with me. I found myself hit with an incredibly strong "fear of missing out," and it made me question if I was doing college the "right way."

Instead of feeling grateful for the friends and experiences I had, I found myself looking for more.

What makes this even more stupid is that I was pitying myself for things I genuinely didn't even care about.

I didn't go out Friday nights because **I didn't want to.** I like my nature walks, and my oversized books, and my long overcomplicated conversations with my roommates.

I *don't* want to spend my Friday night in a sweaty frat house. But because everyone else was doing it, I felt like I was the weird one for not. Somehow I had managed to gaslight myself into *wanting* to leave my house.

This problem was made worse by the fact that I had a small friend group. I adore each of them, but we were just a sum total of four morons.

There was this big scare in the middle of my freshman year where my roommate was thinking of taking a gap semester to chase a genuinely fantastic opportunity in Texas.

This scared me because he was my closest friend at BU and so suddenly the "emotional ground" I stood on became very shaky. What would I do if one of my three core friends just… disappeared?

At the time, he was also the center of our little group, with the rest of us having met through him. So, not only was I losing my roommate and close friend, I might have been losing my bridge to the other two as well.

He didn't end up taking the opportunity, but it made me realize how *vulnerable* I felt about my number of friendships.

I broke out of this illusion by making an **active effort** to meet more people, but in a way that was true to myself.

I started scheduling coffees and lunches with more tertiary friends because that's how I enjoy getting closer with people. I spent more time outside my dorm at various community locations because I'd run into friends I knew from class. I got more involved with clubs and activities and, by virtue of time, I just ended up becoming closer to those people in those communities.

Today I'm much more confident in general because I'm much more confident in my *ability* to make new friends.

There are still many people at BU who have more friends than me. There are still many people at BU who go to parties and post on Instagram.

But... I'm *happy* with the little network I have and my little group of morons.

I'm excited to see who else I meet, but I'm also able to sleep very well at night knowing that the relationships I have cultivated are more than enough.

-----------

My friends think I'm crazy when I tell them about these doubts I have.

Not because these thoughts are silly or unheard of. In fact, many of my friends have felt the same way.

Rather, they think I'm crazy because **it's me** who is telling them these doubts.

My friend in computer engineering once asked me for tips on how to be social. My friend from Washington University told me she really admires the way I pursue and accomplish my own projects. My friend from Northeastern never fails to boast that I'm graduating in three years instead of four. My friend from Notre Dame will impassionedly compliment my writing. My friend from Stevens says I always inspire her after our conversations.

Self-doubt comes from a seed of truth, but it is also as substantive as breath on a mirror. As soon as I look at myself from **any other** person's point of view, I find that I am not doing that badly at all. In fact, I'm doing pretty well.

Comparisons and doubts are things I think I'll deal with for the rest of my life, but I refuse to let them continue to **run** my life. They are important to acknowledge, but shouldn't hold power over me in the long run.

If you experience doubts about yourself, (hobbies, choices, future, etc.), hear them out, but then put them aside.

You'll make progress at your own pace, and one day you'll look back and be astounded that you had those doubts in the first place.

Love,
Treshan

# Subject: Self

Dear Triyana,

After an embarrassingly long time thinking about it, I *think* I finally know who I am.

I know I like jackets and dislike tomatoes. I know I like my friends and love my family. I know that both groups can also really frustrate me.

I know I like raindrops but don't go outside to listen to them. I spend most of my time in my head, even when I'm with you. My grandest travel aspiration is to visit Nebraska, though Japan would be pretty cool. I like books but then I also like logic. I like colors, but I can't color in the lines.

And yet… none of the above actually defines **me** at all.

Tomorrow I can suddenly decide that I hate jackets and love tomatoes. I can decide that I want to visit Nevada over Nebraska, or I can decide that I actually *can* color between the lines.

I can change so dramatically, in such a short time, and still be me.

I used to think that "self" was a goal—a static concept. A place I would reach when I figured everything out.

But in reality, my sense of self is fluid. The person I am today is not the person I will be tomorrow. Who I am now changes with context and the situation. Who I will be changes with what I learn and the way I grow.

And then there are the *contradictions*.

The values I claim to have that I don't actually follow. The frustrating resistance my personality has to be defined by any one set of words or ideas. The wonderful ability to be quiet, loud, selfish, selfless, kind, cruel, smart, and stupid all within the same breath.

It's all so... *messy*.

The question "Who am I?" is very difficult, but maybe that's because it's incomplete. Inside it are a dozen other questions:

- "Who am I now?"
- "Who do I want to be?"
- "Who was I?"
- "Who will I be?"
- "Who do I need to be?"
- "Who should I want to be?"

Discovering and building myself has been a confusing, emotional, and strangely beautiful process—one I don't think I'll ever fully understand.

But I can start to explain *parts* of it. Pieces of insight. Frameworks that helped me make sense of myself, even if only temporarily:

- Perspective
- Values
- Versions

# **Perspective**

College students have an awfully bad habit of getting radicalized. Someone who enters as an incurious agnostic could exit as a die-hard Christian. A born-and-raised Midwestern conservative could exit an unapologetic Marxist. A wide-eyed bleeding-heart activist could exit cynical, cruel, and self-interested.

In truth, "radicalized" is far too strong a word. Students *change* in college. That's the **point**. We go to learn new things, and learning new things means coming out a little different.

Oddly, I don't think my friends have changed all that much; rather, they've just become more of themselves.

Their personalities are sharper, their identities more defined, and their values more clear. As if they were a blurry image that suddenly had the chance to see itself in 4K. Some people have had surprising character arcs, but often those arcs are only surprising because I didn't know the person well enough.

Outwardly, I don't think I've changed all that much. Sure, I dress a little better and talk a little louder, but I don't think the college projection of me is all that surprising compared to the version of me from high school.

Internally, though, I've changed a lot. Much more than I ever expected to, and in a way that has made me so much happier about myself and life.

Admittedly, I think I've been a *little* radicalized here, not towards any specific religion, political party, or dogma. Rather, it's my perspective on the world that has started to change. You see, I'm currently in the process of transitioning from a **pragmatist** to an **idealist**.

A pragmatist is a person who is guided more by practical considerations rather than by ideals. An idealist is a person who is guided more by ideals than by practical considerations. Basically, the idealist focuses on the *principle* of a given action, and a pragmatist focuses on the *outcome* of a given action.

When I was younger, I idealized pragmatic characters in the media I consumed. I liked the robots, the scientists, and the strategists. Always composed, always in control, and nearly always right. Logical supercomputers who could determine the right path forward to achieve their goals, occasionally overriding a little moral stipulation to do so.

As such, I put a lot of emphasis on being hyper-logical and making rational decisions. I tried to live an "optimal" life.

This mindset, while not inherently bad, can lead to some problems.

If my goal is to optimize for pleasure, I could turn to drugs and alcohol and be high till I die. If my goal is to optimize for seeing the world, I could disappear completely and leave my family, friends, and any responsibilities I have. If my goal is to make millions of dollars, I could achieve that by selling weapons to terrorist groups at a high premium.

Those examples were a little extreme. How about some more tame ones?

If my goal is to be financially successful, I could get a high-paying job that I hate and spend 60 hours a week disillusioned and bored. If my goal is to be famous, I could make myself really controversial on social media and use hate comments to boost my engagement. If my goal is to make a big positive impact on the world, then I could sacrifice most of everything (relaxation, time spent on hobbies, time spent with family) in order to build something truly good and impactful.

I struggled to make pragmatic choices because pragmatism doesn't work as well when you have multiple priorities.

Should I optimize for happiness? But happiness is related to multiple variables: comfort, satisfaction, struggle, friendship, etc. If so, which variable should I choose? Should I optimize for all of them? Or is there something else I'm completely missing? Should I just focus on money? But "they" always say money doesn't buy happiness. But maybe it does? I think I'd prefer crying about a scratch on my Ferrari instead of crying about not being able to pay my bills.

The above dilemmas are at the core of my opportunity cost problems. I waste so much time agonizing over achieving the perfect outcome when I'm not even sure about what the perfect outcome looks like.

So, since I was stuck trying to figure out what the perfect outcome should be and how to get there, I focused on the **process**.

I stopped focusing on "Is this club good for my resume?" and instead asked "Do I like being in this club?" I stopped focusing on "Is this a good use of my time?" and instead focused on "Is this making someone's day better?" I stopped focusing on "Will this be good for my future?" and started focusing on "Am I satisfied doing this?"

Now, this doesn't mean that I fully abandoned my pragmatic side. I still do things I don't want to because it's good for my future or better off in the long run. But I have clearer lines and stronger opinions for what I'm willing to do for success and what I'm not willing to do.

Perhaps having strong values makes me a little more naive, but that's exactly the **point**.

Could I make hundreds of thousands of dollars joining a company that blows up children in other countries? Probably. But I hope to high heaven that I'm never so cynical that I actually would.

This new perspective—this idealism, this focus on values and processes, this emphasis on the journey over the destination—is something I believe defines me. It's something I strive for. It's the person I want to become.

# **Values**

The most interesting subquestion of "Who am I?" is "Who do I want to be?"

Who I am right now is not as important as who I'm trying to be for tomorrow. Asking, "Who is the best version of me?" and "What would they do in this situation?" often leads to better outcomes for my decisions than just asking "What should I do?"

I defined the best version of myself by a set of values—characteristics that this version would exemplify, and values this ideal version of me would hold in reverence.

There are five: *Courage, Compassion, Honor, Humility,* and *Patience.*

When I have to make a bigger decision, or I'm unsure of what to do, I weigh that decision against these five values.

For example, let's say I had a huge crush on a girl and wanted to ask her out. Here is how I would approach untangling my emotions using this "values" model.

**Courage,** in this case, would say to go for it. It would say I should throw caution to the wind and try my hand, consequences be damned. It would push me to ask her out and see what happens.

Courage was the first value I established because it is counter to my nature. I'm a cautious person, and so for the past few years, Courage has been pushing me to step out of my comfort zone and grow. Admittedly, I still have a bit of work to do here, but I think I've made progress.

**Compassion** doesn't have too much of a role in *this* decision specifically. I *could* ask myself if it is compassionate to the girl to ask such a significant question. I also *could* factor in if this question is kind to *myself* because I will be opening myself to potential harm.

But both these arguments are stretches of what Compassion is meant to be. This value is meant to spur me to be a kinder person. It is meant to inspire me to help others and always consider others' feelings. This was the last value I added because I think I'm generally an empathetic person. Recently, my arc has been focusing on self-compassion (not being too hard on myself).

**Honor** has a *very* strong voice here. Honor dictates that I tell the girl how I feel because it's the truth. In fact, Honor would take it a step further and encourage me to ask her out properly in person, pay for the dinner, and walk her home at night.

In truth, I treat Honor as a stand in for Integrity: the ability to act truly and honestly. I just really like the word Honor, so I use it instead. This value's job is to push me to live authentically and to live in alignment with the other values. It's kind of like the backbone of the entire system. Be authentic, be accountable, be honorable.

**Humility** would ask what the *reality* of the situation is. It would ask to clear the high emotions, excitement, negative thoughts, and to try to see the full picture. It would try to determine if my excitement was justified, and ask if my doubts were justified. It would help clean the water so I can see *clearly*.

For a long time, I thought humility was the same as self-doubt. I thought because I had low self-esteem I was humble. I now realize that Humility is the ability to see myself or a situation without any embellishments (good or bad). Humility asks me to remember that I'm just me, not a hyper-awesome version of myself created by pride, and equally not a super terrible version of myself created by doubt. It's the quietest of the value system, and enables me to see myself as I truly am.

**Patience** would recommend waiting to get more information. It would recommend continuing to talk to her, try to meet in group settings, and wait for the right moment.

Patience was the second value I added, as a counterbalance to Courage. Since I'm a cautious person, Patience comes more naturally to me, but I'd argue that it's **not** the same thing as caution. Caution is colored by worry, while I see Patience as more of a neutral feeling. The ability to be comfortable even when waiting. It's a deceptively hard value to live up to, especially in the hyper-stimulated environment we are in.

I like these five values because they work well together and balance each other out. Courage and Honor often go hand-in-hand. Courage and Patience are often at odds. Compassion is often enabled by Patience. Humility is the result of Compassion towards myself. Honor requires Humility to judge myself.

I like that this model is flexible; these values can be applied to practically any decision.

It is also forgiving. As long as I make a decision after making these considerations, I'll regret it less because I have *some* reasoning. I'll know **why** I made that decision, I'll know my intentions were good, and I'll know that I made the best decision with the information I had.

# **Versions**

If you think about it, we are different versions of ourselves every moment of our entire lives.

Taking different roles, acting in different ways, doing different things as we move to progress and grow. Sixteen-year-old me was different from eighteen-year-old me, who is different from twenty-year-old me.

I often fall into the trap of believing growth is linear—that the version of me living today is superior to my younger self in every way.

In truth, I find that there is a lot of wisdom in seeing the *strengths* of the past version of me and accepting the *shortcomings* of the current version of myself.

**The Administrator**: I think my high school self had the highest discipline of any version of me. On the hardest days, that madman got up at 6:30 AM for a student government meeting, struggled through a school day packed with AP classes, led an oversized robotics team from 3:30 to 10:00 PM, and then finished his homework by 1:00 AM to restart it all again. He had a list to do and locked in to make sure everything was completed.

**The Dreamer**: My freshman year self constantly reimagined the future. He was ambitious and could visualize the idea better than any other version. He was the one who set the goals in my **Direction letter,** and he was the one who wanted to be an entrepreneur. He couldn't go a few days without having some fantastic idea about *something*. He mocked up a nonprofit organization that would fund charities by selling toiletries, created a constitution for a club focused on self-improvement, and outlined a brand for a creative writing peer-improvement platform.

**The Artist**: In the beginning of sophomore year, I reconnected with my love of writing. This version of myself found an outlet in the words he penned and the ideas he organized. He wrote short stories and poems, learning and developing his creative process. He was the version of me to finally understand that the delineations between short stories, poetry, articles, and essays were quite thin. At the end of the day they were all just words—collections of symbols to convey intent and meaning. This was the version of me who started to see art in everything.

**The Child**: My mom loves to watch old videos of me as a kid. She also loves glancing at me with genuine sadness on her face, pointing to the screen, and asking "What happened?"

I cannot blame her.

The child version of me was *adorable*, but beyond that he was also loud, funny, and expressive. He danced and sang and spun around. He seemed excited by everything around him, pulling from a pool of energy that never seemed to run out. He was social, he was bold, he was authentic.

Yet, of course, each of these versions of me had flaws.

The Administrator was rigid and cold. He only cared about the immediate tasks in front of him and often forgot to smile and live. The Dreamer was scattered and flaky. For all his amazing ideas, he lacked the conviction to follow through on them. The Artist spent far too much time in his head. He forgot that the best art comes from interacting and playing in the real world. The Child was unrefined and uncontrolled, unable to control his anger or understand nuances in the world.

**But** the current version of me can learn something from every version who came before.

When I'm overwhelmed and stressed, I call on the Administrator to calm me down and start knocking off tasks. When I'm dejected and stuck, I call on the Dreamer to reimagine a clever solution. When the world gets a little too gray, I call on the Artist to fully appreciate the nuance and beauty in everything. When I'm doubting and hesitant, I call on the Child to throw caution to the wind and move forward.

I want to take the best of every version of myself—the four I mentioned and every other smaller arc and aspect that make up my history and who I am."

Every part of me contributes; every part of me works together to grow into the best version of myself.

-----------

Love,
Treshan

# Subject: Absurdity

Dear Triyana,

The hard part about listening to college advice is that college is completely absurd.

It's an institution of learning—except it's not about learning; it's actually about building your career and finding a job.

BUT WAIT. It's actually about figuring yourself out and learning how to live your best life.

Actually, no… it's about partying your behind off for four years before you hang your personality out to dry and become a corporate sellout for the next forty years of your life.

The "college experience" somehow manages to wrap up self-betterment, hedonism, conflict, peace, learning, and unlearning all in the same breath and is still somehow **more** than all of those things combined.

There are *so many paths, so many points, so many purposes*. I can say the point of college is self-exploration, while your parents will say it's about getting a job, while a fuzzy-haired academic will say it's about advancing the fringes of human knowledge, while a frat bro will tell you it's about getting laid.

What. The. Actual. F*CK.

I got so lost in trying to figure out what college *should* be.

**Everyone** around me had an opinion. Everyone had thoughts and ideas. I tried to give every single opinion the same consideration, but this just made it really hard to deal with opposing statements.

For a long time, I wished there was just *one perspective* that felt *right*—one perspective that could be my anchor as I navigated everyone else's opinions and expectations.

And... there is.

It's mine.

Well, mine for me anyway. It's your perspective for you. It's your best friend's perspective for her. It's your uncle's perspective for him.

At the end of the day, it's **my life** and I have to figure out what to listen to and what to disregard.

**I'm** the one accountable for my actions. **I'm** the one who has to live with regrets or failings or successes. **I'm** the one who is going to cherish the best of this experience for the rest of my life, and who is going to regret the worst of this experience for the rest of my life.

College is absurd, so explore it the way **you** want to. Work yourself to death, lounge around all day in the sun, devour books, go out to parties, take pictures, run marathons. Do all of it. Do none of it.

There are infinite options, so pick the ones that make sense and feel right in the moment. *Listen* to advice and *then* decide if it's worth following.

Is it weird to say that I've loved everything about my college experience, even the bad parts? Even when I was at my saddest or my most stressed out, I was genuinely happy to be there. College can be depressing, lonely, messy, challenging, yet I've always found it... engaging? formative? satisfying?

I'm very excited to hear what shenanigans you get up to in your freshman year—the parties you attend, the dinners you ravage, the finals you fail, and the incredible things you accomplish.

Here's to a year full of laughs, tears, adventure, and growth.
-----------

Love,
Treshan

# Acknowledgments

Thank you to **Paige Jalosinski** for turning my abstract instructions into an amazing cover design. It's everything I pictured and more. I highly recommend checking out the rest of her art at **paigejaloart.com** or on Instagram at **@paigejaloart**. If you're looking for a creative collaborator, I cannot endorse her enough—her professionalism, flexibility, and artistic vision are unparalleled.

Thank you to **Lucy Levine** for her encouragement and support during the early stages of this project. Had it not been for her enthusiastic validation and thoughtful input at the beginning, I don't think I would have had the courage to pursue this further.

Thank you to **Jon**, **Ksenia**, and **Faidon** for their input on the alpha version, as well as for their friendship, company, and support throughout my college experience. I have no idea how I lucked into finding you three, but I'm endlessly grateful to have had you with me on this journey.

Thank you to **everyone** who acted as a **beta reader** for the book. Your thoughtful feedback helped shape this from a collection of meandering thoughts into a finished, cohesive work. I was genuinely touched by the time and effort you all put in—despite being busy with college, clubs, work, and life.

To my parents, **Dee Nilaweera** and **Ashan Nilaweera**—I cannot thank you enough for the love and support you've given me throughout my life. Without everything you've provided—and continue to provide—I wouldn't have made it to college, let alone found the confidence, skills, or discipline to finish writing a book.

To **Triyana Nilaweera**, thank you for making this project possible. There were several earlier versions of this work, but no matter what I tried, the tone, voice, and vision felt off. It was only when I began addressing these chapters to you that I finally found the clarity and direction I needed to move forward.

**Finally, last but not least—thank you for reading!**

I hope you enjoyed following my journey through college and found the insights in this book helpful.

If you did enjoy it, please consider leaving a review on Amazon.com! It really helps increase visibility and get the book into the hands of others who might benefit from it.

If you'd like to read more of my writing, prose, and poetry, you can find me here:

**Instagram**: @tnilaweeraauthor
**LinkedIn**: treshan-nilaweera
**Substack**: www.twrites.com
**Website**: treshannilaweera.com

Made in the USA
Middletown, DE
11 August 2025